UNITED STATES
OF
AMERICA

CRESCENT

NEW YORK

On a crisp day in 1977, a big jet from Europe touched down at the airport in Bangor, Maine.

Erwin Kreuz, a brewery worker from West Germany, strolled into the terminal building for a sample of the local beer, which he found acceptable; then he set out to see the sights.

Maine is spectacular in October. The forests are scarlet, yellow and orange, the air is crystal clear, and though winter is on the way, Indian summer is still there. Mr Kreuz had obviously picked a perfect time to visit.

He drank it in for three days. But all the while, he had a strange feeling that something was wrong. Something was. He thought he was in San Francisco. There are no cable cars in Bangor, no Golden Gate, no Chinatown, no Fisherman's Wharf, no Nob Hill. They're all 3,000 miles away!

Silhouetted against an orange sunset is the Manhattan skyline **right,** *while the RCA Building dwarfs Paul Manship's huge, golden statue of Prometheus* **above.**

The story has a happy ending, though. They treated him like a king in Maine for a week, then packed him off to the West Coast where the party went on for another week.

His adventure is almost the story of America. Back in 1492, Christopher Columbus discovered it, but he was so sure he was someplace else, he named the natives "Indians". Columbus was out to prove the world was round, and he was certain he could reach the exotic East by sailing west, so it's obvious he thought he was in India. When he realized he wasn't, he moved on.

About 500 years before him, Norsemen led by Leif Ericson apparently stumbled on North America. They called it "Vinland The Good", but didn't think it was good enough either to stay or even make a record of their visit.

There are stories that Swedes and Norwegians came to America from Greenland in the 13th century. And still more that say America was really discovered by the Irish, or the Welsh, or the Chinese, or the Phoenicians. But through it all, none of them seems to have known what they discovered. And none of them cared.

Once it had been discovered, however, people came to explore it. And in almost every case, what they were really looking for was a way *around* it or even *through* it.

Columbus never knew he had discovered a whole new continent, but he found out enough about it to know that it was rich in gold and silver; and to the Spanish who financed his expedition, that was a whole lot better than spices from the Orient or some half-baked theory

The colors of Fall are reflected in the tranquil lakes and rivers of the Eastern seaboard. No artist could completely capture the variation of hues, as the light shimmers through dense foliage to the brilliantly-colored carpet of leaves and bracken below.

CITIES OF THE SKIES

pirates, Sir Walter Raleigh, used his Spanish treasure to start a colony in Virginia. Though his original colony ultimately failed, it did succeed in introducing tobacco to the world and helped the British realize there was, perhaps, more to America than gold and silver.

In the first half of the 17th century Europeans began arriving and settling down. The English set up shop in Jamestown, Virginia, in 1607. A year later the French arrived in Quebec. Twenty years later, the Dutch founded Nieuw Amsterdam, and 10 years after that, the Swedes established a colony in Delaware. The Dutch eased them out rather quickly; then the British moved the Dutch out of their colony and renamed it New York.

A magnificent sunset provides a golden background to the skyline of Houston in Texas **left,** *and highlights the awe-inspiring stainless steel "Gateway Arch" in St. Louis* **lower right.** *Dominating the city, the arch soars 630 feet high. The immense Sears Tower in Chicago* **above** *is the tallest office complex in the world, standing 1468.5 feet, with 110 stories. That the largest complex of this type should stand in Chicago is perhaps appropriate, the city being the birthplace of the skyscraper.* **Top right** *Hartford, the state capital and largest city of Connecticut, is the home of many major insurance and other companies. Its lights twinkle on the waters of the Connecticut River. Manhattan's soaring structures are pictured* **overleaf.**

about the shape of the world. Within 20 years they were exporting a million dollars a year in gold and silver from America, and that encouraged them to look around for more.

In the process they established colonies, including St. Augustine on the Florida peninsula in 1565. It was the first permanent European settlement in the United States. So permanent, it's still there.

Meanwhile, watching Spain's wealth growing encouraged others to explore this new world. French explorers claimed all the territory from the Carolinas north to the St. Lawrence River and settled in Nova Scotia, Florida and South Carolina.

The English got into the act, too. But they found it more fun to raid the Spanish treasure ships than to build towns and farms. One of the

While all this was going on, the French were pushing inland toward the Great Lakes and down the Mississippi to the Gulf of Mexico. The stage was set for war.

There were four wars in all, beginning with one called "King William's War", and ending with one called "The Seven Years War". Oddly enough, none was fought in America, but America was what they were all about. When they

were over, France had lost claim to her American colonies, and England and Spain divided up the country between them. Under the treaty, Spain got all the territory west of the Mississippi and England claimed everything to the east.

The Spaniards thought they had made a good deal. They had found great riches among the Aztecs and Incas in Mexico and South America, and the Indians told them there were "Seven Cities of Gold" to the north. Indeed, a Spanish priest in search of heathens to convert had reported seeing one of them somewhere near where the Arizona–New Mexico border is today. They had been exploring the territory for a century, going as far north as Kansas, as far west as California. They didn't find the "Seven Cities of Gold" – no one ever has – but they were fairly certain they weren't east of the Mississippi.

The British were slow starters in colonizing America, but ultimately their colonies were the most successful. In 1620, just a few years after the founding of the Virginia colony, a group of religious dissenters arrived in Cape Cod Bay, Massa-

HIGHWAYS AND FREEWAYS

In a land where virtually every household owns at least one automobile, highways and freeways snake around and through the cities. Intricate patterns are created in Dallas **top,** *Houston* **above,** *and San Francisco* **right.**

chusetts. As Puritans, life under James I in England had been less than joyous, even to these people who considered "joy" a four-letter word. With the King's blessing 101 of them, and a ship's crew of 48, had set out to escape persecution and to find a new life in the New World.

NEW ENGLAND

Their ship, of course, was the "Mayflower"; their colony, Plymouth, and they are remembered today as "Pilgrims". They were Englishmen first, travelling with the permission of the Crown and at the expense of The London Company, who owned the settlements in Virginia.

Some say they were off course, some say it was a careful plan; but the fact is, they landed far north of the Virginia colony outside the jurisdiction of The London Company. This left them free to make their own rules, and before leaving the ship they drew up a document that became the law of their colony. Basically, it bound them together to voluntarily obey the rule of the majority. It was an almost revolutionary idea in 1620, and it became the first step toward another bigger revolutionary idea, the United States Constitution.

The East Coast of America is steeped in history. **Right** *is a replica of Brig Beaver II, which was used in the notorious Boston Tea Party; the bas-relief* **bottom** *adorns one of the monuments on Boston Common. Chatham Lighthouse, Cape Cod,* **left** *and an old church in Providence, Rhode Island,* **below,** *are just two of the historic buildings which serve as a reminder of colonial days, while Yale University* **center and bottom left** *imparts a sense of timelessness.*

Life was far from easy for the colonists on Cape Cod Bay, but they managed to survive in spite of it. Within 20 years, they had a thriving colony of hard-working souls. A decade later, they had absorbed more than 20,000 in the biggest mass migration England has ever seen. To make room for the newcomers. they started some new towns

NEW YORK

with such names as Cambridge, Charlestown, Gloucester and Boston.

As often happens when oppressed people look for freedom, the Massachusetts settlers didn't give much freedom to people who didn't agree with them. It wasn't long before they had dissenters among themselves, who went down the Cape to start a colony of their own, which they called Rhode Island.

The soil in Massachusetts was poor for farming, so another group set out further south and settled down in Connecticut, which made the Dutch in Nieuw Amsterdam very nervous indeed. More of them went up to the southern coast of Maine, which had already been settled by

The buildings of Manhattan thrust aggressively skywards **right.** *The Empire State Building* **far right below** *remains the symbol of the skyscraper. Dominating the skyline now are the twin towers of the World Trade Center* **above.** *The bronze statue of Atlas* **far right above** *is sited on Fifth Avenue.*

the French, and still more moved west into New Hampshire.

The Indians had been friendly, even helpful, to the colonists, but all this expansion was too much. The Puritans didn't believe in buying territory from the natives; they just marched in and took it. The tribes in Connecticut didn't think

that was right, and so they rebelled by attacking the settlements. In retaliation, a force went out from Massachusetts and wiped out an entire tribe, destroying their villages and capturing survivors to sell as slaves in the West Indies. That solved their immediate problem, but gave them a much bigger one in return. And so to protect themselves from the hostile savages, the colonists bound themselves together in a confederation they called ''New England''.

Meanwhile, people were pouring into the new world from old England. The King was giving away huge tracts of land to both his creditors and his old friends. One of those friends, Sir George

COLOR AND PAGEANTRY

Americans take every opportunity to dress up: from the colorfully-costumed Colonial Williamsburg militia company, which attracts many tourists to its historical displays **top far left, left and bottom left,** *to the fun-filled and spectacular family entertainment at Circus World, near Orlando, which provides a chance to relive the thrills of a bygone era when the circus came to town* **other pictures these pages.**

Calvert, had visited Virginia and liked it very much. But he wasn't allowed to stay because he was a Roman Catholic. The King fixed that by giving him land north of Virginia. Calvert died soon after, and the grant went to his son, the second Lord Baltimore, who named the estate "Maryland", which he established as a colony for English Catholics.

The southern and middle colonies were run almost like feudal estates. The grants decreed that any laws passed should not violate English law

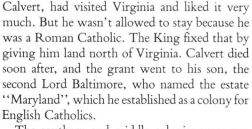

and should have the consent of the people. But the land owners were free to give or sell land to settlers on whatever terms they decided. Baltimore's terms were possibly the most feudal in the entire British Empire, and his colony was slow to grow. He also faced unreasonable anti-Catholicism, and finally the third Lord Baltimore was forced to convert to the Anglican Church to keep control of his grandfather's grant.

Not all the settlers in the English colonies came

LANDMARKS

from England. By the time King Charles II repaid some favors by giving the Carolinas to eight of his cronies, not many Englishmen were eager to leave home. But Barbados and the other British West Indies islands had become very crowded, and some of the planters there were more than happy to migrate north and west. They brought along an institution that would become an American tradition for the next 200 years: slavery.

Once the English had convinced the Dutch that New Netherland was not a healthy place to live, the King gave the territory to his brother, the Duke of York, who in turn gave it his name. He gave the southern part of his grant to two of his friends, who called it ''New Jersey''.

They, in turn, sold part of their land to a group of Quakers, one of whom was William Penn. The land didn't have access to the ocean, so Penn approached the Duke of York, who had taken over a territory to the south on the mistaken assumption that it was part of his grant. Penn bought it from him and established a colony called ''Delaware''.

William Penn's father had been a close friend to, and creditor of, the King. Penn inherited the friendship and the unpaid dept, for which he accepted an American land grant. He set up a colony called ''Pennsylvania'', dedicated to

Man-made and natural beauty: reflected in the waters of the Potomac River Tidal Basin is the graceful Jefferson Memorial **top,** *while the Capitol Building* **right,** *atop Jenkins Hill, is probably the most impressive building in the city of Washington DC. The awesome Horseshoe Falls at Niagara are seen* **above** *in the grip of winter.*

complete religious freedom. Though intended as a refuge for Quakers, he welcomed anyone, and as a result, his was the fastest-growing colony America had yet seen. The Quakers came in huge numbers, along with Mennonites, Baptists, Jews and others. They came from Wales and Scotland and Ireland, from Sweden and from Germany. And they all agreed that they liked what they found there. Even the natives were friendly. Penn was fair-minded to a fault, and made it a point to pay the Indians for their land. He also made treaties that were fair to both sides and made sure that they were backed up. The result was that Pennsylvania farmers, who didn't own guns, lived in complete peace with the Indians while settlers all around them lived in terror of the ''savages''.

It was more than 50 years later that the last of the major English colonies was established when James Oglethorpe set up Georgia as a haven for people from the debtors' prisons in England.

Over the following 40 years, cities grew, farmers and trappers began moving further west and immigrants kept pouring in from all over Europe. By 1760, the population had reached 1,700,000, the country was prosperous and the cities cosmopolitan. A whole continent stretched out to the west waiting to be conquered. But first, the British had to be overcome.

*The "Old South" atmosphere is captured by gracious mansions such as those at Biloxi **left,** and Longwood **center right and below,** in Natchez, Mississippi; Drayton Hall, Charleston, **bottom right,** and Nathaniel Russell House, Charleston – picture **bottom left** shows one of its oval drawing-rooms. Colonial Williamsburg has recreated its 18th-century existence with the preservation of picturesque houses **bottom** and taverns such as Chownings **top right.** The "Natchez" **overleaf** provides a memorable trip on the Mississippi river.*

It started quietly, of course. Most wars do. Word had gone out that the British were going to Lexington in Massachusetts to arrest a pair of rebels named Sam Adams and John Hancock. About 70 patriots, calling themselves "Minutemen", assembled on the village green to take a stand against them. And there, on April 19, 1775, a pistol shot rang out, followed by a volley of rifle fire from the British Redcoats. Within a month, Great Britain was at war with her American colonies. The war would last until 1781, when General George Washington, with the help of the French Marquis de Lafayette, defeated the British forces at Yorktown in Virginia. As

the British marched away, their band played an old march, "The World Turned Upside Down". And for them it had.

For the first time, the American stars and stripes fluttered over a free and independent nation.

That flag had 13 stars; today it has 50. At the time the peace treaty that officially ended the war was signed, the United States covered 800,000 square miles from Maine to Georgia and from the

THE SOUTH

Atlantic to the Mississippi. Today it covers more than 3,600,000. There were about 3 million Americans then. Today the population has grown to more than 203 million.

What is a typical American? There is really no such thing, but combining census statistics, the typical American family would seem to live in a metropolitan suburb at about the point where Wyoming, Montana and South Dakota come together. Since there are no big cities anywhere near there, one can't help being cynical about statistical evidence. But to press on ... the typical American family, according to the census, owns its own home, which is worth about $17,000 (in

a metropolitan suburb!). The family is about 90 percent white, but speaks a little Spanish, looks slightly oriental and has ancestors who were pure American Indians. The man of the house is 44 years old and he's married to a woman who admits to 41. They have 2.35 children, whom they support on an income of $9,867. That makes them affluent enough to own one and a quarter automobiles.

And so on. Every American family appears to own three radios, and more Americans own a TV set than have a bathtub or a shower in their house. They're religious too. Only about 5 percent say they have no religion at all. And of the rest, 66 percent are Protestant, 26 percent are Catholic and 3 percent are Jewish. The other 5 percent are divided among just about every religion known to mankind.

People are fond of calling America a "melting pot". But in the melting process, most of the people who migrated to the United States from

other countries brought a little of the old country with them. It's as common for one American to ask another what nationality he is as to ask about his astrological sign. And some of the answers are amazing. "I'm English-Irish-German and Swedish", one might say. Or the answer might be more simply, "I'm an Italian-American". During political campaigns, it's as common to hear calls for an end to such "hyphenated Americanism" as it is to hear pleas that "no American should go to bed hungry". And with rhetoric like that, it's no wonder only about half the eligible voters ever go to the polls!

But the fact is, most Americans enjoy the sense

*The statue **far left** stands in the Vicksburg National Military Park. The Governor's Mansion, Atlanta **left** and the State Capitol Building in Frankfort, Kentucky **right** are two more examples of fine buildings in the South. Bustling Memphis **below** contrasts with the peace of Shenandoah Valley **below right**.*

of community that comes from sharing their roots. And while many Americans do go to bed hungry, an overwhelming percentage of them are on diets, and the average family in the United States spends more on food alone than the total annual income of the average Greek family.

It's a nation of movers. Some 20 percent look for greener pastures every year, and sometimes the moving almost amounts to a mass migration. In the last 50 years, huge numbers have moved from the South to the North and thousands more have gone the other way. Farm workers have moved to the cities; city folks have moved to the suburbs, and California doesn't ever seem to stop growing.

But the more they move, the more the population centers seem to stay the same. Only about 1.5 percent of the land in the United States is taken up by cities and towns, and more than half the people live close enough to have a Sunday picnic on the shores of the Atlantic or Pacific Oceans, the Gulf of Mexico or one of the Great

FLORIDA

Lakes. It's still very much a country of wide open spaces, and even though only about a quarter of all native-born Americans still live in the state in which they were born, more than a quarter of the total population lives along the Atlantic Coast, about the same percentage that lived there a century ago.

But almost from the beginning, the pull was from the West. After the Revolution, the Spanish still controlled Florida and the land west of the Mississippi. The British had never bothered to leave Ohio, and just about everything west of the original 13 colonies was wilderness occupied by trappers and traders, Indians and a few farmers. A generation later, the United States had bought "Louisiana", an area that began at the Mississippi, went past Texas and stretched west into present-day Montana and Wyoming. It doubled the size of the country and opened vast opportunities for immigrants.

People began taking advantage of the opportunity in the 1820's, when German and Irish immigrants arrived in big numbers, eager for a new life and willing to take a chance on the wild frontier. People who had been born in places like Connecticut and Maryland joined them, lured by the promise of cheap land. Farmers from the already soil-exhausted South picked up stakes and went along, too. Others went in search of adventure, some went to escape debt. But most went West because it was there. It gave them a chance

to start a new life, something Americans are still doing, more than 150 years later.

By the time the migration to the West gained real impetus, there were passable roads across the Appalachian Mountains. The migrants went in Conestoga wagons, in pack trains and in fancy stage coaches. Once across the mountains, the Ohio River took them into Tennessee and Kentucky ... all the way to the Mississippi, in fact, and from there up to the Great Lakes, down to the Gulf of Mexico and across into Missouri and Arkansas.

Their new homes needed to be established in

The glistening beaches and turquoise waters of Miami, Florida **these pages,** *attract many thousands of holidaymakers every year.* **Left** *Hugo and Lolita, the killer whales, make a spectacular leap in the Miami Seaquarium.*

hostile wilderness, populated by Indians who didn't much like seeing their homelands turned into farms and by Europeans who egged the savages on. But those who went into Ohio found signs of a very friendly man who made it his mission in life to make their lives pleasanter.

His name was John Chapman. When he died in the 1830's, the Fort Wayne, Indiana, Sentinel reported:

"Died in the neighborhood of this city, on Tuesday last, Mr. John Chapman, better known as Johnny Appleseed. The deceased was well-known throughout this region by his eccentricity, and the strange garb he usually wore. He followed the occupation of nursery-man".

Remembering Johnny Appleseed as a "nursery-man" is almost the same as remembering George Washington as a "planter". He wandered through the wilderness for more than

TRADITION & TECHNOLOGY

50 years planting apple trees as well as other fruits and medicinal plants he knew would be useful to the settlers who followed him.

He began his wanderings in Pittsburgh, after having planted orchards all the way from Massachusetts to Pennsylvania. Everyone who knew him loved him, even the Indians who were generally hostile to the white men. But even those who loved him most had to agree he cut quite a bizarre figure. They say he wore a coffee sack with holes cut in it for arms, and a stewing kettle passed for a hat. He would appear mysteriously at the door of a settler's cabin to ask for a place to spend the night. When he was welcomed inside, he always refused to sleep anywhere but on the floor and before the sun rose in the morning, he had vanished as silently as he had appeared.

Once, when the city of Mansfield, Ohio, was being attacked by Indians, Chapman ran 30 miles to the nearest fort and was back again with help in less than 24 hours. Another story about him, which may or may not be true, was that he was seen in the woods playing with a family of bear cubs while their mother watched benignly. He always walked barefoot, even in winter, and could find his way anywhere without a compass.

Deeply religious, he led an utterly selfless life. He didn't own a gun, and couldn't hurt a living thing. A legend about him says he once doused a campfire so mosquitoes wouldn't be burned to death in the flame. He wouldn't eat meat, and

The Midwest states, heart of the continent, are the most typical regions of the United States. Best known for their pasturelands dotted with small towns, their cities nevertheless have much to offer. Shown here are Chicago **above**, *Cincinnati* **left**, *and Detroit* **lower left**.

would never accept anything from anyone unless he could exchange it for seeds or a small tree.

When Ohio began to get too "crowded" for him, he moved further west into Indiana where he finally died. For years after, people on the frontier told affectionate stories about this wonderful little man. There were so many stories, in fact, that people who didn't know better began to think there had never been such a person as Johnny Appleseed.

By the time he died, more than a million people had settled in Ohio. Almost 4 million lived west of the Allegheny Mountains, and nine more states, including Illinois, Missouri and Alabama had joined the original 13.

At about the same time, President Monroe decided it was about time to get rid of some of those Indians who stood in the way of expansion. General Andrew Jackson and Indiana's Governor William Henry Harrison, each a future President, had defused the Indian menace on the frontier and a new standing army kept it that way. Now, new treaties dictated that Eastern tribes should move West ahead of the wave of immigrants. The Creeks, Cherokees, Choctaws,

TRADITION & TECHNOLOGY

Chickasaws and Seminoles were all forced to walk what they called "The Trail of Tears" into what the Government called "Indian Territory".

They called it "progress". It's a thing Americans still believe in with unabashed enthusiasm.

From the ornate to the simple – the Bahai House of Worship, Chicago **bottom,** *and St. Gabriel's Catholic Church in Louisiana* **below. Left** *Just two of the many fascinating exhibits at the Kennedy Space Center at Cape Canaveral, the site for the launching of many of America's space explorations.*

No problem is so great that "American ingenuity" can't solve it. America first discovered its courage in these people who moved West in the 19th century. They took civilization into the wilderness and made it work. Long before the century was half over, the country was well on its way, not just to the Pacific Coast, but to a position of importance in the world no country so young had a right to expect.

One of the people who originally explored the land just west of the mountains fired the imagination of would-be frontiersmen and still inspires Americans today. His name was Daniel

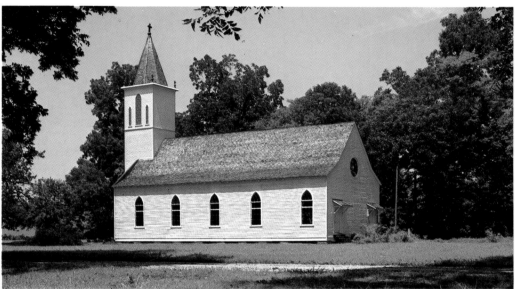

Boone. He was a Pennsylvanian who moved to North Carolina as a boy and spent most of his life exploring Kentucky.

On his first long trip he was captured and robbed by Indians four times and after two years of hunting came back empty-handed. But he loved every minute of the adventure, and he became a master of Indian psychology as well as an enthusiastic hunter and explorer.

His tales of the wilderness encouraged a North Carolina entrepreneur to buy Kentucky and part of Tennessee from the Cherokee Indians. His stories also got him the job of mapping a road through the territory. Once into the interior, he built a town, which he modestly called "Boonesboro". Not long after, he was taken prisoner by Shawnee Indians determined to capture and destroy the settlement. But he talked them out of it and in the process so charmed them that they adopted him into their tribe, changed his name to "Big Turtle", and treated him as the son of their chief.

But all the while, he was still their prisoner.

It was several months before he escaped and got back to Boonesboro to warn his friends the Indians were coming. When they arrived, the

Glistening deep blue lakes, pine forests and craggy mountains; spectacular gorges threaded with ribbons of river; lush meadows full of grazing cattle – Colorado's beautiful Rocky Mountains are a treasure trove. Pictured here are Beaver Ponds in Hidden Valley **left,** *the Black Canyon of the Gunnison* **above right,** *and one of the many herds which roam this magnificent area* **above.**

settlers were ready for them, resolved to fight to the death to save their town.

They nearly had to. The Shawnee kept at it for two months, trying every trick in their book to destroy the settlement. But Boone knew their tricks and so none of them worked. Finally, the Indians tried to tunnel under the stockade. Boone dug a trench in their way, but they kept at it. Then a heavy rain made their tunnel collapse and the Indians went home in disgust.

He had saved his home, but Daniel Boone was never a homebody. Leaving the great ''Wilderness Road'' as a permanent monument, he set out to explore even more of the country. At 65, when people today think of retiring, he joined the Lewis and Clark expedition up the Missouri River and into the Oregon Territory.

He opened the way for people as tough as himself. Men and women with large families of children built cabins in the middle of the woods. They generally cleared 40 acres or so by stripping the bark from trees so they would die. Once dead, it was a simple matter to burn away the trunks and dig out the stumps. They burned the tall grass away so new grass would feed their cattle, and planted grain on the land they had cleared. Women looked after the children, of course, when they weren't cooking, churning, hoeing, spinning, chopping wood or carrying water.

Not everyone lived in the wilderness, though. Great cities were being established, too. Cincinnati, Pittsburgh and Detroit were all lusty and thriving at the beginning of the 19th century, and in a 1795 treaty, the Indians had turned over ''a piece of land six miles square at the mouth of the Chickago River, emptying into the south-west end of Lake Michigan, where a fort formerly stood''. In 1803 a new fort was built there to stand guard over the gateway to the Northwest Territory. Some French traders, holdovers from the days when this was French territory, lived across the river.

The fort was destroyed in the war of 1812, and yet another was built after the war was over. It was a center for the fur trade until the market dropped, and was again reborn as the City of Chicago when a canal was dug over the old portage route the French trappers had used.

New York City has an international flavor that can't be matched by any other city in the world. San Francisco has a classic charm that makes it the favorite of most Americans; Denver has a setting that makes most other cities envious, but no other city is as truly ''American'' as Chicago, Illinois. New York, Boston and Philadelphia were well into their second century when people began settling down along the lake shore. But this city was different. For the first time, possibly in the history of the world, builders asked <u>women</u> what sort of houses they'd like. The answer was loud and clear. They wanted porches and big bay windows and yards that went around all four sides of the house instead of the attached row houses of other cities. They got what they wanted. It was a neighborly place then and it still is.

THE OLD WEST

Chicago is where modern architecture was born and where it exists at its best. It's the city of Frank Lloyd Wright and Mies ven der Rohe and the man who started it all, Louis Sullivan. Sullivan's philosophy was based on the tradition of the early builders who took the trouble to talk with the people who had to use their buildings. He didn't think a bank should look like a fortress or a factory like a tomb. In later years, his ideas would be taken to Europe and sent back as something new. But, as can be seen in the "improvements" in cities like Atlanta and Houston, the switch from "Chicago Style" to "International Style" had a very sterilizing effect on the original idea that "a building is an act".

The good news is that Chicago is alive and well. Anyone on a search for America would do well to begin there. In its early days, once the frontier had pushed that far west, it became the gateway to the Golden West. But the door swung both ways. It also became the gateway to the East and South for the ranchers and farmers from the West, and by the time the Civil War broke out, Chicago was already what Carl Sandberg later called it: "Hog butcher for the world".

When the railroads pushed West, Chicago was at the center of the activity. It still has the biggest railroad terminal in the world and the busiest airport, and it's still the gateway to the Golden West.

The territory north of Chicago: Wisconsin, Michigan, Minnesota and all the way west to Oregon, was a land of logging camps in the early days. Instead of burning out the forests as the pioneers to the south and east had done, they were at work providing the raw material to build a country.

The loggers in the Northwest, the keelboatmen on the Mississippi, the farmers and the builders were all made of tough stuff. There was hard work to be done, and they were the right people for the job. Hard work had been an American tradition right from the start, and they made it look easy.

Another quality Americans have always admired is "rugged individualism". The Yankees in New England respected it as much as their religion, and it went west along with the country.

The historic complex of Dodge City **left, above, top right and center right,** *in the state of Kansas, has been preserved to show it as it was in the late 1800's, a notorious frontier town. Hundreds of pioneers traveled across the continent in transport such as the old Conestoga wagon* **above left. Right** *Cattle are still an important part of the state's wealth and industry. The most famous sight in the Black Hills of South Dakota is the sculpture on Mount Rushmore* **overleaf.** *The heads of Presidents Washington, Jefferson, Lincoln and Theodore Roosevelt were carved as a memorial to the birth, growth, unity and vigor of the United States.*

When Indiana was still an untamed frontier, the territory between the Missouri River and the Spanish missions in California was wild, hostile, unexplored country. It was a perfect setting for the rugged individualists they called "mountain men".

It was all the rage in London and Paris in the 1820's to own soft felt hats made of beaver hair. They were as expensive as they were fashionable, and beaver pelts brought good prices. Trappers, armed with big rifles, pistols, tomahawks and hunting knives ran their lines across the plains and into the Rocky Mountains beyond. In later years, Buffalo Bill made himself the personification of these mountain men, who were the first white men to see the huge herds of buffalo on the plains, the first to ride through the Rockies, the first to fight the Apache and other hostile Indians in the West. They wore big-brimmed hats and fringed leather shirts and pants; their faces were smeared with campfire grease and their hair streamed out behind them as they rode their horses over trails only Indians had ever seen.

They lived their lives in the mountains and on the prairies, slipping back toward the east about once a year to meet traders who went out from St. Louis to meet them and to exchange beaver pelts for whiskey and fresh clothes.

Meanwhile, the Spanish hadn't given up looking for the fabled "Seven Cities of Gold", but by now they had confined their activities to the Southwest from New Mexico and across Texas into California. They had missions and settlements up the California coast from San Diego to

THE OLD WEST

San Francisco. And, as if they didn't have enough troubles in the desert peopled by angry Indians, the Russians were coming.

The Czar was as interested as anyone else in Europe in finding a "Northwest Passage" across North America, and he sent an explorer named Vitus Bering to take a look.

Bering explored Alaska and discovered it was rich in otter, a happy little animal whose fur was very highly-prized in China. That lured trappers from Siberia, who ranged down the coast to within about 50 miles of the Spanish settlement at San Francisco.

The vast Texan landscape displays a variety of scenes, such as the Rio Grande River tumbling into the international waters of Lake Amistad **below,** *and is of course perfect for its important cattle industry. These pictures illustrate the typical scenes at auctions and the popular rodeos.*

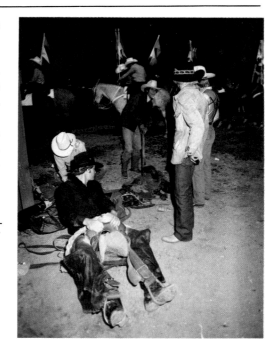

At the same time, British fur traders moved west across Canada. And Americans, including a New Yorker named John Jacob Astor, set up trading posts at the edge of the Oregon territory. The days of Spanish California were clearly numbered.

Back East, Americans were dreaming a new dream. Until then, the lure had been gold or timber or furs. But the American dream was for the land itself. Many of the immigrants from Europe had come from peasant stock, and the

idea of actually owning their own land was almost too good to be true. They came to believe it was their sacred duty to carry civilization west. A New York newspaper told them ... "Our manifest destiny is to overspread and to possess the whole of the continent which Providence has given us for the development of the great experiment of liberty and federated self-government".

That was all they needed!

The major trails began at Independence, Missouri, jumping off place for the Santa Fe Trail into the Southwest or the Oregon Trail that headed north toward the Columbia River. It was a boom town in the 1840's with pioneers arriving with huge families and all their belongings loaded into ox-drawn, canvas-covered wagons. They usually stopped there for a while, buying supplies, hiring a mountain man to guide them and organizing themselves into trains of at least 40 wagons.

They took cattle with them, so they had to wait in Independence until the grass on the prairie was abundant enough to feed the stock. And since they all believed in the code of "rugged individualism", it wasn't easy for them to organize themselves into congenial groups.

Once under way on the Oregon Trail, they found the Kansas and Nebraska countryside beautiful if ominously quiet and desolate. The

THE BIG COUNTRY

Awesome structures like Cathedral Rock in Sedona's Oak Creek Canyon **below left** *are commonplace in Arizona, a state which counts the breathtaking Grand Canyon as one of its main attractions! This view of the Canyon* **right** *was taken from Hopi Point. One of the best-preserved of its kind is the cliff-dwelling of Montezuma Castle* **below,** *well over five hundred years old.*

boredom was often broken by wild rainstorms that washed out their camps and flooded the streams they had to cross.

The wagons travelled four or more abreast so they could be organized into protective squares if Indians attacked. The men walked with the oxen to keep them moving, the boys kept the cattle from straying and the women sat at the front of the wagon, usually knitting.

The going got rougher when they reached Chimney Rock in Western Nebraska and their wagon wheels began to sink into the sandy soil. They were usually out of firewood by then, and as there were no trees to cut, they cooked over buffalo chip fires. Fort Laramie, in Wyoming, offered them a chance to load fresh supplies, to repair their wagons and to steel themselves for the hard part of the trip, the Rockies.

The route across Wyoming toward Idaho was littered with cast-off furniture, abandoned to make the wagons less burdensome for the starving oxen. It was uphill all the way until they reached a pass that took them through the mountains and over the top to find even more hostile, barren country ahead.

If they were lucky enough to make it before winter, they settled down in Oregon and California. And they never looked back. Yet, oddly, even native Californians today refer to everything on the other side of the Mississippi as "back East".

The Oregon Trail was laid out by the Lewis and Clark expedition; the Santa Fe Trail was the route of mule trains and caravans of ox carts that carried American trade from Independence down into New Mexico. It stretched almost 800 miles across the desert and through Apache country, so it wasn't as popular with the early emigrants until gold fever hit them in 1849 and people started heading west for different reasons.

A third major route to the West began in Palmyra, New York, a small town near the Erie Canal. A man named Joseph Smith was plowing his field there one day when an angel, who said his name was Moroni, introduced him to God and His Son.

Smith wrote a book about it, which he called "The Book of Mormon", and started a whole new religion. Some people in Palmyra didn't like the idea and they ran Smith and his followers out

DESERT COUNTRY

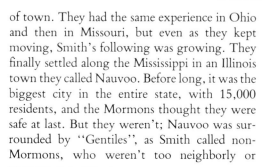

of town. They had the same experience in Ohio and then in Missouri, but even as they kept moving, Smith's following was growing. They finally settled along the Mississippi in an Illinois town they called Nauvoo. Before long, it was the biggest city in the entire state, with 15,000 residents, and the Mormons thought they were safe at last. But they weren't; Nauvoo was surrounded by "Gentiles", as Smith called non-Mormons, who weren't too neighborly or tolerant of these people who were said to practise polygamy. When Smith ordered a newspaper destroyed because it was critical of him, the Gentiles made their move. They lynched Joseph Smith.

Brigham Young became their leader, and he took on the mission of leading his people to a new land where there were no Gentiles. They sold their houses in Nauvoo and built wagons to make a long trip to the Great Salt Lake, which

found was what they themselves created; the Wild West.

Most of the big cattle spreads were in Texas and Colorado, but the Texas ranchers drove their longhorns as far north as the Dakota Territory to fatten them up over the winter before shipping them to the slaughterhouses in Chicago. The cowboys who drove them a thousand miles north were a lusty lot who spent 16 hours a day in the saddle, choking on dust, watching out for marauding Indians, heading off stampedes and fighting rustlers and armed farmers who didn't like to see all those cows trampling their crops.

A trail drive averaged about 2,500 head of cattle which were driven an average of 1,500 miles. A trail boss, in charge of about a dozen cowboys and a cook, was completely responsible for the operation, and shared the profits once the cattle were sold. His cowhands were paid about $30 a month and board.

Fourth highest in the United States is the Glen Canyon Dam **far left. Right and far right** *Pueblo Indians, of which there are more than 20,000 in New Mexico, are well-served by their own cultural center in New Albuquerque, the downtown area of which is seen under a full moon* **top left.** *Located in Santa Fe is the First Presbyterian Church* **left,** *while Shiprock Peak* **above,** *sharply outlined against a glowing sunset, stands aloof and gaunt.*

---

had been discovered some years before by Western explorers.

A few had oxen to pull their wagons, but most loaded their belongings into hand carts and started the long walk west. By the fall of 1847, some 2,000 of them had reached the ''Promised Land'', but what they found there was a dry, sun-baked plain. They put themselves completely under the control of their church, and together made the valley bloom. Meanwhile, thousands of converts arrived from the East and from Europe, and a string of settlements sprang up. There were enough of them before long for Brigham Young to announce that they had established an independent nation. He called it ''Deseret''. The U.S. Government called it the Territory of Utah, but it took 50 years for them to make the idea stick.

Even the Civil War didn't slow down the rush to the West. In the year General Sherman marched through Georgia, some 75,000 people marched in wagon trains along the Oregon Trail. And after the war ended in 1865, freed slaves and war veterans poured across the Mississippi looking for adventure and opportunity. What they

Naturally, all that work made them thirsty. The cowtowns along their routes obliged them with plenty to drink as well as friendly games of chance to help boost their income, and companionship to boost their morale. It was a tough life, often a short one, but to be a cowboy in the Wild West is still an American boy's fondest dream.

Cowboys, gunslingers and U.S. Marshals were only part of the population who tamed the Wild West, however. In 1862, President Lincoln signed a law that entitled any American citizen (or anyone who intended to become one) to 160 acres of land for nothing more than a small filing fee and a promise to live there and farm it for at least five years. Civil War veterans went by the thousands into Kansas and Nebraska, the Dakotas and Montana to take the Government up on its offer. Europeans were lured by the promise of a free farm, too, and in less than a generation the country's population doubled. The cowboys called the Homesteaders ''Sod-busters''. The law required them to be farmers, but the farms got in the way of the cattle drives. The Indians didn't like their fenced-in acres either, but they were clearly there to stay.

The cowboys and Indians had another enemy, too. Sheep herders. After the Spanish brought sheep to California, the Indians themselves helped spread herds into Colorado and Texas. By the time the "Sod-busters" began arriving, the "Woolies" had half a million head of sheep on the range and were at war with the cattle ranchers. One range war in Arizona lasted more than

five years, and before it ended more than 30 men died. Up in Wyoming one night, masked men attacked four sheep camps, tied up the shepherds and clubbed 8,000 sheep to death.

In yet another scheme to encourage settlement of the West, the Government gave millions of acres of land to the railroads that were being built through the territory. The railroad companies mounted an advertising blitz telling Easterners, "You Need A Farm!" and thousands agreed. They carried their campaign into Europe, and Germans, Dutch, Swedes, Norwegians and

The rich, vibrant atmosphere of Texas is characterized perhaps by the use of Houston as a site for the NASA Space Center **right and below.** *Relaxation is provided in the many recreation areas and sports centers such as the Summit Stadium* **bottom left** *and the University of Texas stadium* **left.** *Harris County Domed Stadium* **far left top and bottom** *is the home of the Houston Astros.*

The diversity of American architecture is illustrated on these pages. **Top left** *is Austin, Texas, dominated by the pink granite State Capitol Building, contrasting sharply with the high-rise blocks of Houston* **left,** *seen here transformed by a million glittering lights. The stately city of St. Paul, Minnesota, is viewed from an icy Mississippi river* **right,** *while summer greenery surrounds Cincinnati* **above.**

Danes responded enthusiastically. In Minnesota and the Dakotas, the Scandinavian languages became more common than English.

So many people flowed into the West that the Government decided it was time to relocate the "Indian Territory". They forced the Creeks and Seminoles to sell some of their land and they called it "Oklahoma". On April 22, 1889, it was declared open under the Homestead Act, and before noon on that day almost 2 million acres had been claimed. Before the sun set, the cities of Guthrie and Oklahoma City had been established. Four years later, the Government bought out the Cherokee territory and 100,000 people moved in on the first day it was declared open.

Meanwhile, people were starving in Ireland; the political situation in Germany was driving people away, and in less than 30 years, beginning in 1831, 3,500,000 people from those two countries decided to become Americans. At the same time, another 1,500,000 migrated from other countries.

Between 1855 and 1890, more than 7 million arrived from Europe through New York alone! They kept coming for more than 60 years after that, and between 1890 and 1954, when the immigration laws were changed, 20 million people from just about every country in the world came to put their mark on America.

By 1872, it was apparent that expansion was dramatically changing the shape of the land. The Mountain men wouldn't have recognized their lonely territory, and the old frontiers in Ohio and Tennessee were completely tamed. To preserve some of the natural beauty of the land, the Government set aside a tract of more than 3,470 square miles (an area bigger than the Commonwealth of Puerto Rico), in Wyoming, Montana and Idaho, and called it Yellowstone National Park. It's the oldest and still the biggest of the

CELEBRATION

country's 37 National Parks. Yellowstone hasn't changed much since hunters, trappers and Indians roamed there more than 200 years ago. It's wild country with moose, elk and more, including a huge population of bears. The territory is laced with geysers and natural hot springs, some with temperatures as high as 200°F. The best known, Old Faithful, sends a jet of water and steam 200 feet into the air every 65 minutes, as regular as clockwork. It's as much a symbol of America to many people as the Statue of Liberty.

Yellowstone straddles the Continental Divide, a range of high mountains that separates East from West. Rivers from the east of it flow toward the Atlantic; from the west, water flows towards the Pacific. Further north in Montana, and spilling across the Canadian border, the

Continental Divide is at its spectacular best in Glacier National Park. It's home to bighorn sheep and grizzly bears and snow that never melts. It was named for the glaciers that carved its breathtaking valleys, but there are still glaciers there, and it's as much like Alaska as any other spot in the lower 48 States.

Daniel Boone would still recognize the country's most-visited National Park, the Great Smoky Mountains in North Carolina and Tennessee. He'd know the restored log buildings and split rail fences, he'd probably stop for a chat with the local blacksmith or pick up some corn meal at the gristmill. But he'd be a little surprised to find nature trails for cars. Actually, though, if he thought about it, he'd smile to think that the

majority of the 8 million people who tour the Park every year never get out of their cars and that leaves the mountaintops and winding trails quiet and peaceful. It makes it possible to explore in the same way he did and possibly not run into anyone else doing the same thing.

Americans are very attached to their cars and rarely go anywhere without them. The result is that many see America as superhighways carefully designed to carry traffic around the small towns and big cities, with interchanges full of ugly gas stations, tacky motels and fast food stands. Others in search of America fly over it in big jets and hope there are no clouds over the Grand Canyon to ruin the view.

It's a part of America that exists, there's no

denying it. But there's another America out there. And it's worth exploring.

Way out West in the wilds of New Mexico, there's a roadside oasis that's a combination gas station, general store, restaurant, meat market and dance hall. On Friday nights, folks drop in for a little companionship, a little gossip, a little

Parades and carnivals are an important part of American tradition, the Thanksgiving Day parades being probably the best known. Celebrated on the fourth Thursday in November, Thanksgiving Day was originally instituted in 1621, and was declared an official national holiday in 1863 by President Lincoln.

something to eat and a few beers. Some of them travel as far as 100 miles for the pleasure, because people are few and far between out there. The population is 0.3 persons per square mile, in fact.

The Friday night get-togethers are repeated in dozens of places along the old cattle driving routes. They were generally spaced about a day's drive apart and usually boasted a well. Today they

SCENIC BEAUTY

The exquisite, jewel-like Crater Lake **right** was created by the eruption and collapse of the stratovolcano, Mazama. The lake is just one of the many wonders to be found in the beautiful state of Oregon. The state of Washington contains majestic scenery too – the azure lake **above** is in the Olympic National Park. Further south is the Yosemite National Park in California, where spectacular sights, such as the towering cliff, El Capitan **top,** can be seen.